ELEPHANTS

by JoAnn Early Macken

Reading consultant: Susan Nations, M.Ed., author/literacy coach/consultant

WEEKLY WR READER®
EARLY LEARNING LIBRARY

Please visit our web site at: www.earlyliteracy.cc
For a free color catalog describing Weekly Reader® Early Learning Library's
list of high-quality books, call 1-877-445-5824 (USA) or 1-800-387-3178 (Canada).
Weekly Reader® Early Learning Library's fax: (414) 336-0164.

Library of Congress Cataloging-in-Publication Data

Macken, JoAnn Early, 1953-
    Elephants / by JoAnn Early Macken.
       p. cm. — (Animals I see at the zoo)
    Summary: Photographs and simple text introduce the physical characteristics
and behavior of elephants, one of many animals kept in zoos.
    Includes bibliographical references and index.
    ISBN 0-8368-3268-X (lib. bdg.)
    ISBN 0-8368-3281-7 (softcover)
    1. Elephants—Juvenile literature. [1. Elephants.   2. Zoo animals.] I. Title.
QL737.P98M32   2002
599.67—dc21   2002016858

This edition first published in 2002 by
Weekly Reader® Early Learning Library
330 West Olive Street, Suite 100
Milwaukee, WI 53212 USA

Copyright © 2002 by Weekly Reader® Early Learning Library

Art direction: Tammy Gruenewald
Production: Susan Ashley
Photo research: Diane Laska-Swanke
Graphic design: Katherine A. Goedheer

Photo credits: Cover © Joe McDonald/Visuals Unlimited; title, pp. 5, 7, 13, 15, 21 © James P. Rowan;
p. 9 © Kim Fennema/Visuals Unlimited; pp. 11, 19 © Gerald & Buff Corsi/Visuals Unlimited; p. 17
© Tom Uhlman/Visuals Unlimited

Printed in the United States of America

1 2 3 4 5 6 7 8 9 06 05 04 03 02

Note to Educators and Parents

Reading is such an exciting adventure for young children! They are beginning to integrate their oral language skills with written language. To encourage children along the path to early literacy, books must be colorful, engaging, and interesting; they should invite the young reader to explore both the print and the pictures.

Animals I See at the Zoo is a new series designed to help children read about twelve fascinating animals. In each book, young readers will learn interesting facts about the featured animal.

Each book is specially designed to support the young reader in the reading process. The familiar topics are appealing to young children and invite them to read — and re-read — again and again. The full-color photographs and enhanced text further support the student during the reading process.

In addition to serving as wonderful picture books in schools, libraries, homes, and other places where children learn to love reading, these books are specifically intended to be read within an instructional guided reading group. This small group setting allows beginning readers to work with a fluent adult model as they make meaning from the text. After children develop fluency with the text and content, the book can be read independently. Children and adults alike will find these books supportive, engaging, and fun!

— Susan Nations, M.Ed., author, literacy coach, and consultant in literacy development

I like to go to
the zoo. I see
elephants at
the zoo.

5

Elephants are huge. An elephant can be as heavy as a school bus.

Elephants use their trunks to eat. They pick up grass and fruit with their trunks.

They use their trunks to pull branches off trees. They eat the leaves and the bark.

Elephants drink a lot of water. They pick up water with their trunks.

Elephants spray dust on their backs to protect their skin from the Sun.

When elephants
are hot, they
spray water
on themselves
to cool off.

Elephants have large ears. They flap their ears to cool off, too.

I like to see elephants at the zoo. Do you?

Glossary

flap — to move back and forth

spray — to sprinkle or send out in tiny drops

trunks — long snouts

For More Information

Books

Arnold, Carolyn. *Elephant*. New York: Morrow Junior Books, 1993.

Macken, JoAnn Early. *African Animals*. *Animal Worlds* (series). Milwaukee: Gareth Stevens, 2002.

Shahan, Sherry. *Feeding Time at the Zoo*. New York: Random House, 2000.

Web Sites

NATIONALGEOGRAPHIC.COM

www.nationalgeographic.com/kids/creature_feature/ 0103/elephants.html

For fun facts, video, audio, a map, and a postcard

Canadian Museum of Nature

www.nature.ca/notebooks/english/afeleph.htm

www.nature.ca/notebooks/english/aseleph.htm

For African and Asian elephant illustrations and facts

Index

About the Author

JoAnn Early Macken is the author of a rhyming picture book, *Cats on Judy*, and *Animal Worlds*, a series of nonfiction picture books about animals and their habitats. Her poems have been published or accepted by *Ladybug*, *Spider*, *Highlights for Children*, and an anthology, *Stories from Where We Live: The Great Lakes*. A winner of the Barbara Juster Esbensen 2000 Poetry Teaching Award, she teaches poetry writing. She lives in Wisconsin with her husband and their two sons.